ENGLAND '66

ENGLAND '66

THE 1966 WORLD CUP IN PHOTOGRAPHS

RAY TEDMAN

Reynolds & Hearn Ltd
London

First published in 2010 by
Reynolds & Hearn Ltd
61a Priory Road
Kew Gardens
Richmond
Surrey TW9 3DH

WORLD CUP '66 CREDITS: 7 Redferns/Getty Images, 8 Getty Images, 12 Popperfoto/Getty Images, 13 Getty Images, 17 Getty Images, 18-19 SSPL/Getty Images, 20 (top) Getty Images, (bottom) Popperfoto/Getty Images, 21 Popperfoto/ Getty Images, 22 Popperfoto/Getty Images, 23 Popperfoto/Getty Images, 24 Popperfoto/Getty Images, 25 Popperfoto/ Getty Images, 26 Getty Images, 27 (top) Getty Images, (bottom) Popperfoto/Getty Images, 28 Getty Images, 29 Getty Images, 30 Getty Images, 31 Popperfoto/Getty Images, 32 Getty Images, 33 Getty Images, 34-5 Getty Images, 36-7 Getty Images, 38 Getty Images, 39 Getty Images, 41 Popperfoto/Getty Images, 42 Popperfoto/Getty Images, 43 Getty Images, 44-5 Getty Images, 46 Popperfoto/Getty Images, 47 Getty Images, 48 Getty Images, 49 Getty Images, 50-1 Getty Images, 52-3 Popperfoto/Getty Images, 54-5 Popperfoto/Getty Images, 56 (top) Popperfoto/Getty Images, (bottom) Getty Images, 57 Popperfoto/Getty Images, 58 Popperfoto/Getty Images, 59 (top) Popperfoto/Getty Images, (bottom) Getty Images, 60 Getty Images, 61 (top) Getty Images, (bottom) Popperfoto/Getty Images, 62 Getty Images, 63 Popperfoto/Getty Images, 64 Getty Images, 65 Popperfoto/Getty Images, 66 Popperfoto/Getty Images, 67 Getty Images, 68 Getty Images, 69 Popperfoto/Getty Images, 71 Getty Images, 72 Getty Images, 73 (top, middle) Getty Images, (bottom) Popperfoto/Getty Images, 74 Popperfoto/Getty Images, 75 Getty Images, 76 (top) Getty Images, (bottom) Popperfoto/Getty Images, 77 Popperfoto/Getty Images, 78 Getty Images, 79 Getty Images, 80 Popperfoto/Getty Images, 81 Popperfoto/Getty Images, 82-3 Getty Images, 84 Popperfoto/Getty Images, 85 SSPL/Getty Images, 86-7 Popperfoto/Getty Images, 88 Popperfoto/Getty Images, 90 Popperfoto/Getty Images, 91 Popperfoto/Getty Images, 92 Getty Images, 93 Popperfoto/ Getty Images, 94-5 Popperfoto/Getty Images, 96 Getty Images, 97 Getty Images, 98-9 Getty Images, 100 Getty Images, 101 Getty Images, 102 Getty Images, 103 Popperfoto/Getty Images, 104-5 Getty Images, 108 Getty Images, 109 Popperfoto/Getty Images, 110 Popperfoto/Getty Images, 111 Getty Images, 112 Popperfoto/Getty Images, 113 Popperfoto/Getty Images, 114 Popperfoto/Gety Images, 115 Popperfoto/Getty Images, 116 Popperfoto/Getty Images, 117 Popperfoto/Getty Images, 118 Popperfoto/Getty Images, 119 Popperfoto/Getty Images, 120-1 Popperfoto/Getty Images, 122 Getty Images, 123 Popperfoto/Getty Images, 124-5 Popperfoto/Getty Images, 126-7 Popperfoto/Getty Images, 128-9 Popperfoto/Getty Images, 130-1 Popperfoto/Getty Images, 132-3 Getty Images, 134 Getty Images, 135 Getty Images, 136-7 Popperfoto/Getty Images, 138 Getty Images, 139 (top) Popperfoto/Getty Images, (bottom) Getty Images, 140 Popperfoto/Getty Images, 141 Popperfoto/Getty Images, 142-3 Getty Images, 144 Popperfoto/Getty Images, 145 Getty Images, 146-7 Getty Images, 148-9 Popperfoto/Getty Images, 150-1 Popperfoto/Getty Images, 152 Getty Images, 153 Popperfoto/Getty Images.

I'd like to thank Jeff Bench for his work on the captions and his many helpful suggestions. Any errors are mine.
Ray Tedman,Spain, April 2010

A CIP catalogue record for this book is available from the British Library.

ISBN 978 1 904674 16 0

Designed by James King

Printed and bound in Malta by Melita Press

CONTENTS

ONE:
SETTING THE SCENE

'I think England will win the World Cup in 1966. We have the ability,
strength, character and, perhaps above all, players with the right temperament.
Such thoughts must be put to the public, and particularly to the players,
so that confidence can be built up'
Alf Ramsey, official press conference, 21 August 1963

'We began to believe in him when he showed that he believed in us.
That seed was sown when he first said "England will win the World Cup".
He came to regret it because it put himself and his players under great pressures.
In fact it built up within us the very confidence we needed'
Bobby Moore

In 1960, when FIFA chose England as the host nation for the 1966 World Cup, to mark the centenary of the standardisation of football by the Football Association in 1863, no-one could have predicted the enormous changes that would take place in British society and the radical changes to football that would follow England's victory on that July summer afternoon.

At the beginning of the decade the Beatles were formed (although their definitive line-up was not to appear until 1962). By 1966, when they released perhaps their finest album *Revolver,* they had taken the world by storm and had become the most influential singer-songwriters in the second half of the twentieth century. The very same year, Bob Dylan – who had been inspired by the Beatles to add an electric sound to his own music – released his definitive double album *Blonde on Blonde.*

England's other young world
beating team of 1966

Klaus Voorman's classic cover design
to the Beatles' album *Revolver*
epitomized the mood of the times

ENGLAND '66

In British society, the 1960s were to provide a break with the preceding post-war years. The late 1950s saw the country breaking away from austerity, with prime minister Harold Macmillan presiding over a period of economic growth and low unemployment (in July 1957 Macmillan told the nation that they had 'never had it so good'). But in its final years the Conservative government was rocked by the Vassall and Profumo scandals which seemed to many to symbolize moral decay and hypocrisy at the heart of the British establishment. In the October 1964 general election the Labour Party, under Harold Wilson, squeezed into power with a majority of four seats. At the party's 1963 annual conference, Wilson had made his famous speech, on the necessity of change brought about by scientific and technological developments (and by implication the necessity of political change) in which he argued that 'the Britain that is going to be forged in the white heat of this revolution will be no place for restrictive practices or for outdated measures on either side of industry.'

By 1966 Labour's popularity had surged, leading Wilson to call a general election which Labour won with a substantial majority of 94 in March of that year.

Increasing affluence and a loosening of so-called traditional values, particularly among the young, led to another revolution – this time a cultural one. By the mid-1960s the phenomenon of Swinging London was well under way. The cover story of US news magazine *Time* dated 15 April 1966 was 'London: The Swinging City'. This passage gives a flavour of the article:

> Britain has lost an empire and lightened a pound. In the process, it has also recovered a lightness of heart lost during the weighty centuries of world leadership. Much of the world still thinks of Britain as the land of Victorianism, but Victorianism was only a temporary aberration in the British character, which is basically less inhibited than most. London today is, in many ways, like the cheerful, violent, lusty town of William Shakespeare, one of whose happiest songs is about 'a lover and his lass, that o'er the green cornfield did pass.' It is no coincidence that critics describe London's vibrant theatre as being in the midst of a second Elizabethan era, that one number on the Rolling Stones' newest LP is a mock-Elizabethan ballad with a harpsichord and a dulcimer for accompaniment, or that Italian novelist Alberto Moravia describes the British cinema today as 'undergoing a renaissance'.

This renaissance was marked in 1966 by the release of three films which encapsulated the changes in British society. *Alfie*, starring Michael Caine, was the story of a young working class man from the East End of London (which, in reality, was Caine's background). Alfie is a Casanova figure, using women for his immediate pleasure, casually abandoning them, leaving a trail of emotional disaster in his wake. Alfie is quite content with his life as long as the 'birds' are in 'beautiful condition' as he confides to the audience.

Morgan – a Suitable Case for Treatment, directed by Karel Reisz, is the story of Morgan Delt, artist, fantasist and socialist, who embarks on a series of increasingly wild schemes to prevent his ex-wife re-marrying, used the context of Swinging London to frame his story. The cast

Alfie – Michael Caine co-stars with Shelley Winters

reflected this context – David Warner (Morgan) had just played Hamlet at Stratford at the age of 24, Vanessa Redgrave (Leonie, Morgan's ex-wife), from the famous acting family and Robert Stephens (Leonie's intended), a star at the newly established National Theatre.

The final film of the trio was made by Italian director Michaelanglo Antonioni. *Blow-Up* records a day in the life a young working-class fashion photographer (a character based, loosely, on 1960s icon David Bailey). The film is part murder mystery, part a reflection on the nature of truth. Perhaps because he saw with the eye of an outsider, Antonioni produced a vivid image of the trendy, anarchic, hedonistic world of London in the mid-1960s. *Blow-Up* starred (again) Vanessa Redgrave – she was to appear in three major releases in 1966 – and David Hemmings, another of the new stars of the 1960s and part of the swinging London scene.

So, you might ask, what did Alfred Ernest Ramsey, born in a small cottage in Dagenham and 40 years old (*40!!!!*) in 1960, have to do with the Swinging Sixties? Well, perhaps, quite a bit. Alf Ramsey, a man from a poor, working-class family, became the manager who took England to World Cup victory, and, for better or ill, had a long-lasting effect on the way that the professional game was played both at home and around the world. In his way, although instinctively cautious and even conservative, Ramsey as revolutionary as the Beatles or their spiritual counterparts The Rolling Stones.

Ramsey started his career as a professional footballer in 1946, as a right back with Second Division Southampton. Although football was his passion, he wasn't a 'natural' – but he was a worker. He developed his skills and in 1948 was included in the England squad, playing his first representative game for the English League against the Irish League in September of the same year. He played his first full international against Switzerland in December (England won 6-0) and kept his place for a further 31 matches.

In 1949 an injury meant that Ramsey lost his first team place, and when, although he had recovered his fitness there still wasn't a place for him in the first team, he asked for a transfer. Tottenham Hotspur stepped in and with an offer of cash and their winger Ernie Jones which meant that Alf's transfer cost the princely sum of £21,000 – the highest sum yet paid for a full back.

Ramsey's career flourished both as a league and international player. But, by 1953, and at the age of 31 (although he claimed to be only 28) his career as a player was nearing its end. His last international, a friendly against Hungary on 25 November, marked the end of innocence for English soccer. Undefeated for 80 years on home soil by non-domestic national teams, England lost 6-3. The seismic shock of the defeat was amplified by an aftershock of even greater magnitude when, on 23 May 1954 Hungary beat England 7-1 in Budapest. Player Bobby Robson said of the first match:

> We saw a style of play, a system of play that we had never seen before. None of these players meant anything to us. We didn't know about Puskás. All these fantastic players, they were men from Mars as far as we were concerned. They were coming to England, England had never been beaten at Wembley - this would be a 3-0, 4-0 maybe even 5-0 demolition of a small country who were just coming

into European football. They called Puskás the 'Galloping Major' because he was in the army – how could this guy serving for the Hungarian army come to Wembley and rifle us to defeat? But the way they played, their technical brilliance and expertise - our WM formation(3-2-2-3) was kyboshed in 90 minutes of football. The game had a profound effect, not just on myself but on all of us. ...That one game alone changed our thinking. We thought we would demolish this team – England at Wembley, we are the masters, they are the pupils. It was absolutely the other way.

Alf continued to play for Spurs, earning £1000 a year, a good wage in the 1950s. Knowing his playing career was approaching its end, he was keen to join the coaching staff but was told nothing could be found for him. Denied a place in the team's 1955 continental tour, the only road for a man whose life was football was management.

As it happened, Ipswich Town, recently demoted to the Third Division (South), needed a manager and Alf, released from his Tottenham contract, got the job. As was his character, Alf applied himself totally to the job. It took him two years to take Ipswich back to the Second Division, and three further seasons to make Ipswich Second Division Champions and win promotion to the First Division. In his seven years at Ipswich he spent around £30,000 on players – extraordinary when you consider his own 1949 transfer fee was £21,000.

Because he was football-obsessed, Alf knew that the 3-2-5 system – so engrained in English football – simply didn't cut the mustard any more. The best teams were trying all sorts of line-ups. He also knew that to change would only work if he convinced the players. 'Any method of play demands complete understanding of what you, as manager, are trying to introduce and they, the players, will have to do to make it work.'

Ipswich and Alf's success had been noticed at the FA's Lancaster Gate headquarters. In the years following the Hungary debacles, England's star had reached its nadir in popular perception – from 'the best in the world' to possibly (and equally absurdly) the worst. The record of the England team was simply mediocre. They were actually joint favourites in the 1958 World Cup in Sweden – Brazil won and England failed to get past their first round. In 1962 England reached the quarter finals of the World Cup in Brazil. However they were comprehensively outplayed by the 1958 winners and, even at FA headquarters, it was recognised that something had to change. Walter Winterbottom, England manager since 1947, departed to the Central Council of Physical Recreation. In many ways he had been a skilled practitioner of the managerial arts but he worked under many restraints, the main one being that he had no say over team selection. That had been, for many years, the responsibility of the FA's International Selection Committee. Sir Stanley Rous, FA secretary 1934-61, described the proceedings of the committee:

The committee of up to 12 would discuss each position in turn and vote on it if necessary. Invariably personal preferences intruded and positions were considered in isolation rather than thought being given to the team as an entity. A typical exchange might start with Major Keys saying: 'But you cannot include Ronnie

Alf Ramsey speaks to members of the England squad, September 1965

Alf Ramsey celebrates his World Cup victory

Clayton. The last time I saw him play, our own half-back looked much more impressive.' Then another would add: 'Yes – when we played Blackburn he wasn't in the same class as ours.'

Winterbottom would explain the reasoning for his selection, but that was generally ignored. It was amazing that the England reality check in the game against Hungary in 1953 had been delayed for so long.

In spite of a popular groundswell in favour of Ramsey as a replacement for Winterbottom, the FA first approached Jimmy Adamson, manager of Burnley. He'd assisted Walter Winterbottom in Chile and, because of that and his friendship with Winterbottom, Adamson saw the England manager's job (under the existing regime) as a poisoned chalice. He turned them down flat – as someone said, at least at Turf Moor he got to pick the team.

And so it was that at the beginning of October1962 the FA wrote to John Cobbold at Ipswich saying that that Alf Ramsey was their candidate as England manager. The board agreed to release Ramsey - if he decided he wanted the job. Alf was definitely interested but it took nearly a month of negotiation before, on 25 October it was announced that he had taken the job, at a salary of £4500 a year.

Alf's duties were as follows:
● Produce the general English training programme
● Arrange squad training
● Work with the FA's new Director of Coaching
● Win the World Cup
● Be responsible for team selection

And so it was that the tectonic plates of the FA finally shifted to produce a new footballing landscape for England football. The dinosaur that was the International Selection Committee was still able to lash its tail in its dying moments, producing England teams that lost to Scotland (2-1, April 1963), France (5-2, May 1963) with a draw against Brazil (1-1, May 1963). Then the beast was dead and our hero was free to select the team that he wanted...

The England team took off for a European tour later in May, winning all three games. When captain Jimmy Armfield was injured in the first match against Czechoslovakia, Alf replaced him with West Ham half-Back Bobby Moore who at the age of 22 was England's youngest ever captain. The results (Czechoslovakia 4-2, East Germany 2-1, and Switzerland 8-1) using the 4-2-4 system announced that Ramsey was in charge. Although Armfield returned to the captain's role when he recovered from injury, the die had been cast.

On 23 October 1963 the Football Association celebrated its centenary with a friendly match against a 'rest of the world eleven', or at least those FIFA had been able to persuade to play. Nevertheless it was a decent squad that England beat 2-1 using a modified 4-2-4 system. A month later Northern Ireland were given the treatment, losing 8-3 at Wembley. It was left to

Scotland, the old enemy, to administer a sharp slap of reality when they won 1-0 in April 1964. But, as Alf pointed out: 'Scotland scored with the kind of goal you don't expect in this class of football.'

Nevertheless, it was a timely reality check. In May the England squad left for an extended tour of Portugal, Ireland and the USA, followed by a 'Little World Cup' series in Brazil. It went fine at first. England beat Portugal 4-3, followed by the Republic of Ireland and administered a 10-0 thrashing of the US (sweet vengeance). Then, after a lengthy flight to Brazil, England faced Brazil in the cauldron of the Macaranca Stadium. Brazil won 5-1. This was followed by a 1-1 draw with the same Portugal side they had beaten three weeks earlier and a 1-0 defeat at the hands of Argentina, who went on to win the competition by beating Brazil 3-0. England came bottom of the four team table. Alf said in a massive understatement 'We know now that there is a gap in our respective standards of football but it is not one that cannot be bridged.' He had slightly more than two years to bridge that gap.

The England manager knew that he had to assemble a squad of the strongest players who had the skills and the motivation to do his bidding. He started to build the foundations by offering Booby Moore the permanent captaincy. Ramsey said: 'He's representing me on the field. There is another Alf Ramsey on the field in terms of Bobby Moore.' But there was still a long way to go before the glittering structure of a winning World Cup team was unveiled.

In May 1965 England beat Hungary 1-0 at Wembley. Gracious as ever Alf commented: 'I am disappointed that we didn't score as many goals as Hungary scored against us in 1953. We could have turned that 1953 score right round and beaten Hungary by it.'

Gradually Ramsey drew new members into the squad – the Charlton brothers, 23-year old Norbert 'Nobby' Stiles. In the 1965 Scotland match England's defensive line was– for the first time – Gordon Banks in goal, George Cohen and Ramon Wilson at right- and left-back, with Bobby Moore and Jack Charlton in the middle. The result was a 2-2 draw, with Scotland drawing level after two England players left the field injured. The injury to 'Budgie' Byrne, a regular player for the past 18 months, put him out of consideration for the World Cup squad and he never played for England again. Byrne's injury led Alf to call up Blackpool's 19-year-old Alan Ball.

On 8 December 1965 England played a friendly against Spain in Madrid's Bernebau. stadium. The England line up was:

Banks

Cohen Charlton J Moore Wilson

Ball Stiles Eastham

Hunt Baker Charlton R

With not a winger among them, playing a 4-3-3 formation, England coasted to a 2-0 win. Bobby Moore said later:

"'til then there had been a recognised winger or two in the side. But that night was born England's 'wingless wonders', with overlapping from behind and a volume of

blind-side running. Here was the modern all-action game which
gave Alf what he considered to be the best of both worlds."

Alf continued to experiment with players and tactics. On 3 July 1966, just before England's
final international (against Denmark), he announced the 22 players who would make up the
World Cup Squad:

	DOB	CLUB
1 GK Gordon Banks	30 Dec 1937	Leicester City
2 DF George Cohen	22 Oct 1939	Fulham
3 DF Ray Wilson	17 Dec 1934	Everton
4 MD Nobby Stiles	8 May 1942	Manchester United
5 DF Jack Charlton	8 May 1935	Leeds United
6 DF Bobby Moore	12 Apr 1941	West Ham United
7 MD Alan Ball	12 May 1945	Blackpool
8 FW Jimmy Greaves	20 Feb 1940	Tottenham Hotspur
9 MD Bobby Charlton	11 Oct 1937	Manchester United
10 FW Geoff Hurst	8 Dec 1941	West Ham United
11 FW John Connelly	18 Jul 1938	Manchester United
12 GK Ron Springett	22 Jul 1935	Sheffield Wednesday
13 GK Peter Bonetti	7 Sep 1941	Chelsea
14 DF Jimmy Armfield	21 Sep 1935	Blackpool
15 DF Gerry Byrne	29 Aug 1938	Liverpool
16 FW Martin Peters	8 Nov 1943	West Ham United
17 MD Ron Flowers	28 Jul 1934	Wolverhampton Wanderers
18 MD Norman Hunter	29 Oct 1943	Leeds United
19 MD Terry Paine	23 Mar 1939	Southampton
20 MD Ian Callaghan	10 Apr 1942	Liverpool
21 FW Roger Hunt	20 Jul 1938	Liverpool
22 FW George Eastham	23 Sep 1936	Arsenal

Ramsey assembled his squad at the Hendon Hall Hotel on 7 July 1966. Until the morning of
Monday 11 July, the day of England's first group match against Uruguay, none of the players
(except Booby Moore) knew who was playing. Then the squad was announced:

G Banks, GR Cohen, R Wilson, NP Stiles, J Charlton, RFC Moore (Captain),
AJ Ball, JP Greaves, R Charlton, R Hunt, JM Connelly

After the years of stunning success and agonising failure, planning, anxiety and belief
it was game on.

A triumphant Alf Ramsay meets with Prime Minister
Harold Wilson and Minister for Sport Denis Howell

TWO:
PRELIMINARIES

The 1966 World Cup was the subject of bitter disagreement before a ball was ever kicked. Sixteen African nations boycotted the tournament in protest against a 1964 FIFA ruling requiring the champion team from the African zone to enter a playoff against the winners of either the Asian or the Oceania zone in order to win a place at the finals. The African nations felt that winning their zone should have been enough in itself to merit qualification for the finals. FIFA finally ruled that ten teams from Europe would qualify, along with four from South America, one from Asia and one from North and Central America.

The format of the 1966 competition was the same as in 1962. The 14 teams which had come through the qualification process, plus England (hosts) and Brazil (champions) were divided into four groups of four. The top two teams in each group advanced to the quarter-finals. The draw for the final tournament, on 6 January 1966 at the Royal Garden Hotel in London, was the first to be televised.

A bit of fun before the serious business gets under way! Stewardesses from British European Airways model the strips of the competing teams in the 1966 World Cup

Group One was based in London, and comprised England, France, Mexico and Uruguay. All the matches bar one were played at Wembley (the exception was the France-Mexico game, which was played at White City stadium).

Group Two was based in Birmingham (Villa Park) and Sheffield (Hillsborough). It comprised Argentina, Spain, Switzerland and West Germany.

Group Three was based in Liverpool and Manchester, and comprised Brazil, Bulgaria, Hungary and Portugal.

Group Four was based in Sunderland and Middlesborough, and comprised Chile, Italy, North Korea and the Soviet Union. Groups Three and Four were to provide most of the shocks and upsets of the Group stage.

Trainer Harold Shepherdson, Alf Ramsay – and the England team that won the World Cup

The England team that won the World Cup. Back row: trainer Harold
Shepherdson, Cohen, Peters, Banks, Ball, Moore, Stiles.
Front row: Bobby Charlton, Hunt, Hurst, Wilson, Jackie Charlton

The French team pictured before their match with Uruguay

The Uruguay team before their group match with France

Argentina's players and officials prepare to leave Buenos Aires

Members of the Argentine team relax
after arriving in London. Left to right:
Tarabini, Marzolini, Varacks, Rattin, Mas

Spain, before the start of one of their group matches

The West German team. This photo was taken before their semi-final match with the USSR

The Brazilian squad training at Lymm Grammar school in Cheshire

The Brazilian squad and their manager Vincente Feola pose together outside their hotel

The Brazilian team before their first group match. Back row: Santos, Denilson, Bellini, Gilmar, Altair, Henrique; front row trainer and physio Americo, Garrincha, Lima, Alcindo, Pele, Jairzinho

The Brazilian team before the start of their match with Bulgaria

Bulgarian goalkeeper Simeon Simeonov trains with his
team in their grounds of their hotel in Chester

Training talk from Bulgarian coach Rudolf Vytlacil

The USSR team. This photo was taken before their semi-final with West Germany

The Hungarian team training in the
grounds of their hotel in Southport

The Chilean squad in training

Members of the Chilean team arrive
at Newcastle railway station, prior to
their group matches

The Swiss team gather outside their hotel in Sheffield

The North Korean squad relax by watching Laurel & Hardy's *Towed in a Hole*

Thumbs down to Brazil! The North Korean team assemble in front of their incorrectly labelled team bus

The North Korean team encounter a local religious figure before the start of their group matches

THREE:
GROUP MATCHES

Despite achieving record attendances for the time, 1966 was a World Cup with few goals. Defensive team formations and tactics favouring high work rates over individual flair were held to be responsible. This attritional style of football was exemplified by England, as they finished top of Group 1 by scoring only four goals, but conceding none. Uruguay were the other team to qualify from that group at the expense of both Mexico and France. All the group's matches were played at Wembley Stadium, apart from the match between Uruguay and France, which took place at White City Stadium.

West Germany and Argentina qualified from Group 2, both finishing the group with 5 points. Spain managed only 2, and Switzerland crashed out of the competition after losing all three group matches.

Up in Lancashire, at Old Trafford and Goodison Park, Group 3 saw the World Champions Brazil finish in a lowly third place behind both Portugal and Hungary – thus being eliminated along with Bulgaria. Brazil's defeats by Hungary and Portugal were both highly controversial, the Brazilians finding themselves on the receiving end of some aggressive tackling that seemed designed to neutralize their attacking flair. Portugal, appearing in the finals for the first time, won all three of their games in the group stage. Their star player was their striker Eusébio, who scored nine goals to make him the tournament's top scorer.

Group 4, based in the North-East, provided the biggest upset of all when North Korea beat Italy 1-0 at Ayresome Park, Middlesbrough. The mystery team from North Korea therefore qualified for the quarter finals at the expense of their illustrious opponents. The USSR finished at the top of Group 4, while Chile finished at the bottom. What further upsets might the presence of an African team have caused?

England 0 Uruguay 0 was the less-than-stellar outcome for the hosts in their opening group match

Uruguay's goalkeeper Mazurkievicz leaps to gather the ball from Jackie Charlton. Jimmy Greaves and Roger Hunt look on

John Connelly fails to penetrate the solid Uruguay
defence during England's opening group match

A pitch invasion by Mexican fans interrupts
Mexico's match against France

Ignacio Calderon leaps athletically but unsuccessfully in an attempt to stop
Bobby Charlton putting England 1-0 ahead in their group match with Mexico

Gordon Banks moves to intercept a cross, while Jack Charlton and Ray Wilson look on

Nobby Stiles clashes with Robert Budzynski during the England-France group game

Ian Callaghan, in his only World Cup appearance, gets the ball away from Simon of France

Ray Wilson tackles Philippe Gondet during England's 2-0 defeat of France

England's Roger Hunt celebrates his goal against France

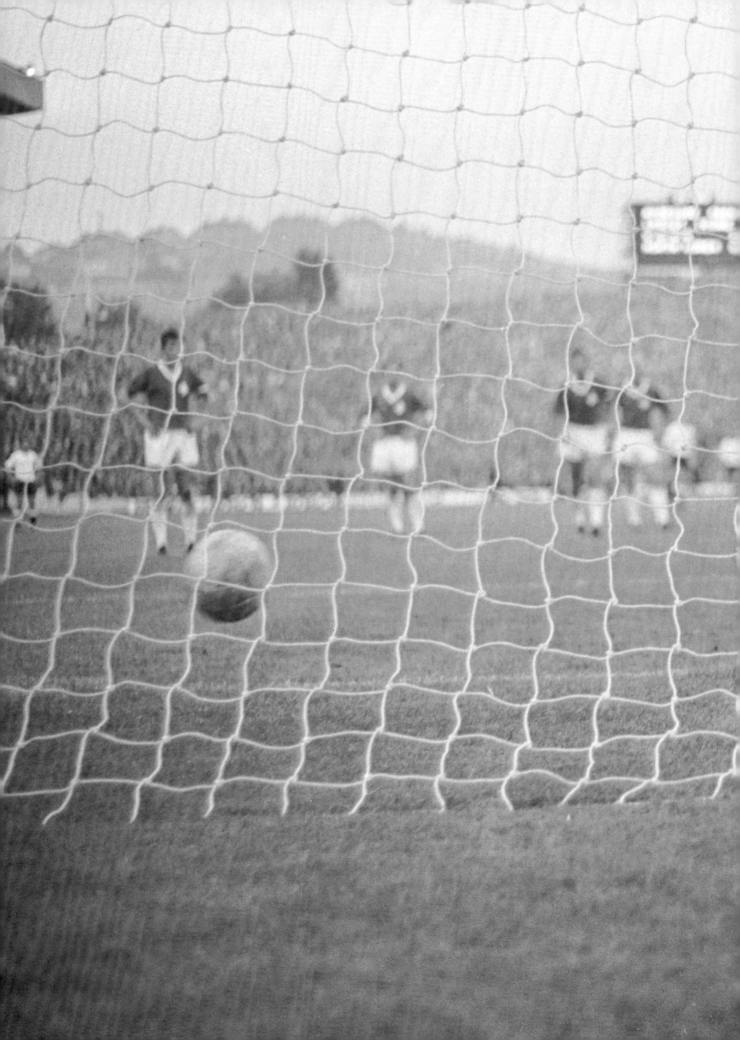

Helmut Haller puts his penalty shot past Charles Elsener, to make the scoreline 5-0 in West Germany's favour in their group encounter with Switzerland

Elsener saves a shot from Seeler

Wolfgang Weber and Jorge Solano compete for the ball during West Germany's encounter with Argentina. Weber's lunge is eerily reminiscent of his equalizing strike against England in the final

Jorge Albrecht of Argentina leaves the pitch after being sent off in the match against West Germany. Argentina's captain Antonio Rattin is still protesting to the Yugoslav referee Konstantin Yecevic

Referee Konstantin Yecevic leaves the field after the West Germany-Argentina match

West Germany versus Argentina.
The game ended in a 0-0 draw

Spain's Iribar jumps against West German captain Uwe Seeler

Spanish defender Zoco blocks a shot from Held during the Spain-West German group match

West Germany 2 Spain 1. Uwe Seeler leaps as Spanish goalkeeper Iribar holds onto the ball

Garrincha scores for Brazil against Bulgaria. Bulgarian goalkeeper Georgi Naidenov leaps in vain for the ball

Pele in action against Hungary at Goodison Park

Hungarian goalkeeper Jozsef Gelei stymies a Brazilian attack
during the group match at Goodison Park

Brazil versus Hungary. Jairzinho is blocked by Beno Kaposzta and goalkeeper Jozsef Gelei

Eusebio leaps to head the ball in Portugal's the match with Brazil

Pele outjumps the Portuguese defence

Pele goes down injured during his country's match with Portugal

Pele leaves he field injured during Brazil's 3-1
defeat at the hands of Portugal

The Italian team line up before their match with North Korea

North Korea get ready to face Italy

Ik shoots from 20 yards

Pak Doo Ik scores the only goal of the match in North Korea's defeat of Italy

North Korean goalkeeper Li Chan Myung clears under pressure
from Italy's Ramono Fogli and Marino Perani

North Korea celebrate their win over Italy

FOUR:
QUARTER-FINALS

PORTUGAL 5   NORTH KOREA 3
23 July 1966. Goodison Park, Liverpool

WEST GERMANY 4   URUGUAY 0
23 July 1966. Hillsborough Stadium, Sheffield

SOVIET UNION 2   HUNGARY 1
23 July 1966. Roker Park, Sunderland

ENGLAND 1   ARGENTINA 0
23 July 1966. Wembley Stadium, London

The quarter-finals provided their fair share of controversy, as well as some of the best action of the entire tournament. West Germany's 4-0 defeat of Uruguay became controversial due to the English referee Jim Finney failing to punish a goal-line handball by the Germen defender Schnellinger, as well as his sending off of two members of the Uruguay team, Horacio Troche and Héctor Silva. Surprise package of the tournament North Korea raced into a 3–0 lead over Portugal after 22 minutes, with goals from Seung-Zin Pak, Dong-Woon Lee and Seung-Kook Yang. The top goal scorer and individual star of the tournament, Eusebio, turned the match around, scoring four goals out of Portugal's tally of five, José Augusto adding the fifth. One of the smallest crowds of the World Cup was treated to a feast of attacking football, with the North Koreans continuing to attack even after going 3–0 up, rather than sitting on their advantage and trying to kill the game.

Ferenc Bene scored a late consolation goal for Hungary against the USSR, but otherwise the USSR's star goalkeeper Lev Yashin repelled everything the Hungarians could throw at him. Igor Chislenko and Valery Porkuyan scored for the USSR. England's ill-tempered clash with Argentina ended with a 1–0 victory to the host nation, courtesy of Geoff Hurst's first World Cup goal. Hurst's winner, after 78 minutes, put England into the semi-finals – and kicked off a rancorous footballing rivalry that has lasted ever since. Argentina's captain Antonio Rattín was controversially sent off for dissent, by German referee Rudolf Kreitlein, 30 minutes into the game. The first player to be dismissed in a senior international football match at Wembley, Rattín at first refused to leave the field. He eventually had to be escorted away by several policemen. The game is still referred to as 'el robo del siglo' ('the robbery of the century') in Argentina.

Augusto heads home Portugal's fifth and final goal, during their thrilling quarter-final clash with North Korea. After falling behind 3-0 after 22 minutes, the Portuguese fought back via four goals from Euseubio. North Korean goalkeeper Ri Chan Hyang can only look on here as the Portugal's fifth is headed home.

The Uruguay squad arrive in Sheffield for their quarter-final match with West Germany

Seeler is brought down

Tilkowski makes a dramatic save
from a Uruguay arrack

Seeler leaps to head the ball as Emmerich watches

Geoff Hurst shoots for goal

Jack Charlton goes down, after a collision with Argentina's goalkeeper Antonio Roma

Bobby Moore and Antonio Rattin lead out their respective
teams, before the start of the tempestuous England-
Argentina quarter-final

Banks punches the ball away during an Argentine attack. Peters and Stiles look on...

Jack Charlton goes down, after a collision
with Argentina's goalkeeper Antonio Roma

The German Referee Rudolf Kreitlin moves to send off
Argentina's captain Antonio Rattin, for dissent...

Rattin refuses to leave the field. These were the days before red and yellow cards were introduced,
and it has been is suggested that – irrespective of his views on the justice of the referee's decision –
Rattin did not at first understand that he had been ordered off the field of play.

Jack Charlton takes the weight off his feet during
the fracas following the dismissal of Rattin

The entire Argentine team prepare to leave the pitch. Play was held up for
nine minutes during their protest over the sending-off of their captain

Geoff Hurst heads the winning goal past Argentina's Antonio Roma

Hurst and Hunt celebrate
Hurst's winning goal

Police and officials escort Rudolf Kreitlin from the pitch at the end of the match

West German defender Schultz shows his relief as the ball flies over the crossbar during a Soviet attack

FIVE:

SEMI-FINALS AND THIRD PLACE PLAY-OFF

SEMI-FINALS

WEST GERMANY 2   SOVIET UNION 1

25 July 1966. Goodison Park, Liverpool

ENGLAND 2   PORTUGAL 1

26 July 1966. Wembley Stadium, London

THIRD PLACE PLAY-OFF

PORTUGAL 2   SOVIET UNION 1

28 July 1966. Wembley Stadium, London

The first semi-final between West Germany and the Soviet Union was played at Goodison Park in Liverpool. Franz Beckenbauer scored the winning goal for West Germany as they beat the USSR.

The second semi-final between England and Portugal was controversially moved at the last moment from Liverpool to Wembley. Bobby Charlton scored both goals in England's 2-1 win. Portugal's goal came courtesy of Eusebio from the penalty spot in the 82nd minute, after Jack Charlton had handled the ball on the goal line.

Portugal went on to beat the USSR 2-1 in the third-place play-off, the winner from Torres coming in the 89th minute.

West German captain Uwe Seeler takes a
flying leap over Soviet goalie Lev Yashin

Stiles and Eusebio compete in an aerial duel

Eusebio leaps high above
Stiles to win an aerial duel

Eusebio and Stiles

Bobby Charlton strikes, to put England into a 2-0 lead – and on-course for the final

Bobby Charlton's crucial second goal

Charlton celebrates his second (and winning) goal in the England-Portugal semi-final

Gordon Banks dives the wrong way, and fails to save Eusebio's penalty strike –
making the score England 2, Portugal 1

Banks and Stiles are still celebrating, while Moore seems to already have his mind on the forthcoming final, and Eusebio is starting to ponder what might have been...

Moore, Stiles, Bobby Charlton, Banks, Hunt, Hurst and Jack Charlton celebrate England's progression into the final - and express their relief, following the tense final minutes of the Portugal game

The disappointment of semi-final elimination begins to sink in for Eusebio

The Third Place Play-Off. Eusebio's shot is saved by Yashin

Anatoli Banishevski and Eduard Malofeyev celebrate
after Malofeyev scores the Soviet Union's equaliser

Eusebio puts Portugal into a winning 2-1 lead from the penalty spot

FIVE:

THE FINAL

ENGLAND V. WEST GERMANY

30 July 1966 Wembley Stadium

THE TEAMS

ENGLAND	WEST GERMANY
1 Gordon Banks	**1** Hans Tilkowski
2 George Cohen	**2** Horst-Dieter Höttges
5 Jack Charlton	**5** Willi Schulz
6 Bobby Moore (captain)	**6** Wolfgang Weber
3 Ray Wilson	**3** Karl-Heinz Schnellinger
4 Nobby Stiles	**4** Franz Beckenbauer
7 Alan Ball	**12** Wolfgang Overath
9 Bobby Charlton	**8** Helmut Haller
16 Martin Peters	**9** Uwe Seeler (captain)
10 Geoff Hurst	**10** Siegfried Held
21 Roger Hunt	**11** Lothar Emmerich

England won the toss and elected to kick off. During the opening minutes, both teams sparred rather nervously with each other. After twelve minutes, Held sent a cross into the English penalty area which Wilson misdirected into the path of Haller, who was dead on target with his strike. The shot flew past Charlton and beat Banks. West Germany had taken an early lead.

Curiously (or perhaps not) the setback seemed to calm England's nerves, and they pressed for a quick equaliser. In the 19th minute, Overath conceded a free kick. Moore floated the ball into the German box, and Hurst deflected the ball into the net for an equaliser.

The score remained at 1-1 until half time, and continued that way well past the hour and into the final 15 minutes of normal time. After 77 minutes England won a corner. Alan Ball delivered the ball to Hurst, who shot from the edge of the penalty area. His shot was deflected by a defender and landed almost at the feet of Martin Peters. Peters beat Tilkowski with his eight-yard shot, to put England ahead for the first time in the match.

The Germans pressed hard for an equaliser during the final minutes of normal time, and in the last minute the referee awarded a free-kick when Uwe Seeler backed into Jack Charlton. Charlton protested that he was in reality the player who had been fouled. The free kick was taken by Emmerich. The ball was blocked by Cohen, but bounced back across the England six-yard box, where Weber lunged with his right foot and connected handsomely to beat Banks, levelling the score and taking the match into extra time. Weber's goal was perhaps the second most controversial in a game of disputed goals, as Banks and the England defenders maintained that Schnellinger had handled the ball during the melee leading up to Weber's final shot.

So the match went to extra time – the first World Cup Final to do so. After eleven minutes, Ball made a break down the right wing and crossed to Hurst, who pivoted and shot from close range. Hurst's strike hit the underside of the cross bar, bounced down – apparently on or just over the line – and was cleared. Referee Gottfried Dienst was unsighted, and consulted his linesman Tofik Bakhramov, who awarded England the goal. England's third goal has remained a controversial one ever since, and footage posted of it can still arouse heated passions in internet chatrooms, decades after the event.

Happily for England, the scoreline did not remain at 3-2. In the final minute of extra time, as the German team pressed forward to try to snatch their second last-minute equaliser of the game, Bobby Moore picked out Geoff Hurst with a long pass. Hurst – pursued by Overath – closed in on the German goal, while some over-excited spectators spilled onto the pitch. Hurst unleashed a ferocious shot that rocketed past Tilkowski into the top left corner of the net. Now it *was* all over – England had won the World Cup. Hurst later mischievously suggested that his blistering shot was a miscue, and that his real intention had been to blast the ball high up into the stands to kill time. But perhaps he was just kidding…?

Booby Moore was presented with the Jules Rimet trophy by the Her Majesty the Queen, and the celebrations began. Some would say that they have never quite stopped. The only achievement that could overshadow 30 July 1966 for England supporters would be another World Cup victory.

Here's hoping…

The teams emerge onto the Wembley pitch

England supporters waving the Union Flag. These days the
Flag of St George is a more common sight at England matches.

The toss. Left to right: West German captain Uwe
Seeler, linesman Tofik Bakhramov, referee Gottfried
Dienst, linesman Dr Karol Balba, England captain
Bobby Moore.

Uwe Seeler, Tofik Bakhramov,
Gottfried Dienst and Bobby Moore.

Haller opens the scoring after 12 minutes,
to put West Germany 1-0 on the lead.

ENGLAND '66

After 18 minutes, Geoff Hurst converts a Bobby Moore free kick to put England level at 1-1

Bobby Moore and Lothar Emmerich

ENGLAND '66

Bobby Charlton evades a tackle

Beckenbauer clears an English shot as Held looks on

Weber and Peters jump for the ball

Tilkowski saves from Bobby Charlton

Emmerich and Moore look on as
Banks punches the ball away

Cohen takes the power of Held's shot full in the chest

Tilkowski saves from Geoff Hurst

Overath can only look on as Peters puts England ahead for the first time after 77 minutes

Emmerich lines up to take the crucial West German free kick, in the last minute of normal time.

Weber drives home the rebound in the confusion following Emmerich's free kick.
West Germany have pulled back to 2-2, with less than a minute of normal time remaining.

The German team celebrate their last-minute equaliser.

The eleventh minute of extra time. Ball crosses
from the right and Hurst shoots on the turn

Weber, Hunt and Tilkowski see the ball bounce around the German goalmouth.

Appeals ring out from both teams after England's controversial third goal. Unsighted, the referee consults with linesman Bakhramov, and the goal is given.

The Germans protest, but the goal stands. England lead 3-2.

Geoff Hurst's blistering shot takes England into a decisive 4-2 lead in the dying seconds of the match. 'They think it's all over... it is now!'

Geoff Hurst and Alan Ball celebrate England's decisive fourth goal

Bobby Moore receives the Jules Rimet trophy from Queen Elizabeth

A smiling Jack Charlton gives a
piggyback to George Cohen

The England team with the Jules Rimet trophy

The celebrations are just beginning...

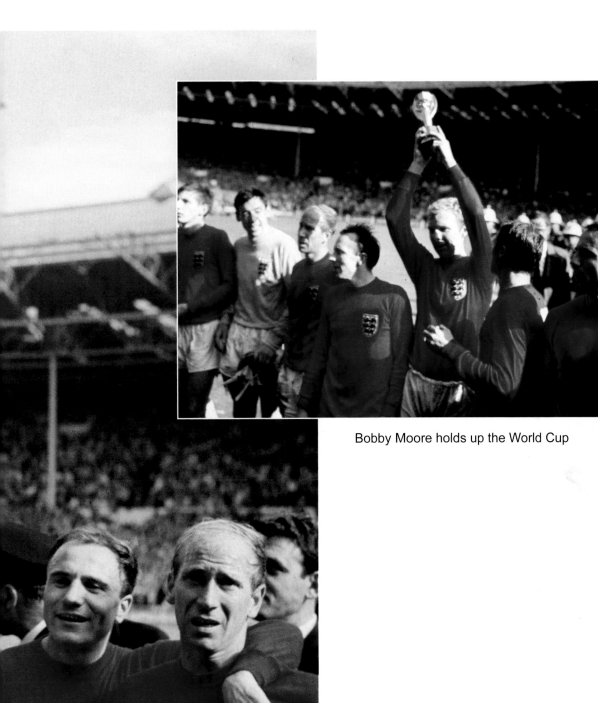

Bobby Moore holds up the World Cup

The triumph begins to sink in. Left to right: Jack Charlton, Nobby Stiles, Gordon Banks, Alan Ball, Martin Peters, Roger Hunt (partly hidden), Geoff Hurst, Ray Wilson, George Cohen, Bobby Charlton

ENGLAND '66

Alf Ramsey and Bobby Moore hold the World Cup

SEVEN:
AFTERWORD

To the victors the spoils – or at least a celebratory reception and banquet at the Royal Garden Hotel attended by the other three quarter-finalists, Prime Minister Harold Wilson, two other cabinet minsters, James Callaghan and George Brown, and a vast squad of FA officials. Wives and girlfriends were not invited but dined in a side room 'like country house servants' in the words of sportswriter Roger Hutchinson. Alf Ramsey was awarded a knighthood in the 1967 New Year's Honours List.

The post-victory glow continued but it never shone as brightly. Sir Alf took an arguably better England team to the 1970 World Cup in Mexico. They reached the quarter finals but were defeated by West Germany 3-2 in extra time, after taking an early 2-0 lead.

The 1974 World Cup was to be held in West Germany. To get to the finals England had to get through a qualifying group. The glow was finally extinguished when Norman Hunter (playing in Bobby Moore's old position) made a fundamental mistake in England's crucial final match at home to Poland, and let Domarski put one past goalkeeper Peter Shilton. England equalised through Clarke's penalty, but a draw was not enough. They were out.

There had been growing criticism of Alf's management style and of the kind of stodgy football that was its result and this was compounded by the failure to qualify. Although during his period as manager the team had lost only 17 out of 113 matches, his employers the FA weren't sentimental – they sacked him on 1 May 1974. He was 54 years old. He never managed a football team again.

England did not reappear at the World Cup finals again until 1982. An era was well and truly over.

EIGHT:
RESULTS

FIRST ROUND

GROUP 1

Team	Pld	W	D	L	GF	GA	GAv	Pts
England	3	2	1	0	4	0	∞	5
Uruguay	3	1	2	0	2	1	2.00	4
Mexico	3	0	2	1	1	3	0.33	2
France	3	0	1	2	2	5	0.40	1

11 July 1966
19:30 BST
England 0 – 0 Uruguay
Wembley Stadium, London
Attendance: 87,000
Referee: Istvan Zsolt (Hungary)

13 July 1966
19:30 BST
France 1 – 1 Mexico
Wembley Stadium, London
Attendance: 69,000
Referee: Menachem Ashkenazi (Israel)
Hausser 62'
Borja 48'

15 July 1966
19:30 BST
Uruguay 2 – 1 France
White City Stadium, London
Attendance: 40,000
Referee: Karol Galba (Czechoslovakia)
Rocha 26', Cortés 31'
De Bourgoing 15' (pen.)

16 July 1966
15:00 BST
England 2 – 0 Mexico
Wembley Stadium, London
Attendance: 92,000
Referee: Concetto Lo Bello (Italy)
B. Charlton 37', Hunt 75'

19 July 1966
16:30 BST
Mexico 0 – 0 Uruguay
Wembley Stadium, London
Attendance: 61,000
Referee: Bertil Lööw (Sweden)

20 July 1966
19:30 BST
England 2 – 0 France
Wembley Stadium, London
Attendance: 98,000
Referee: Arturo Yamasaki (Peru)
Hunt 38', 75'

GROUP 2

Team	Pld	W	D	L	GF	GA	GAv	Pts
West Germany	3	2	1	0	7	1	7.00	5
Argentina	3	2	1	0	4	1	4.00	5
Spain	3	1	0	2	4	5	0.80	2
Switzerland	3	0	0	3	1	9	0.11	0

West Germany was placed first
due to superior goal average.

12 July 1966 19:30 BST
West Germany 5 – 0 Switzerland
Hillsborough Stadium, Sheffield
Attendance: 36,000
Referee: Hugh Phillips (Scotland)
Held 16', Haller 21', 77' (pen.),
Beckenbauer 40', 52'

13 July 1966
19:30 BST
Argentina 2 – 1 Spain
Villa Park, Birmingham
Attendance: 48,000
Referee: Dimiter Rumentchev (Bulgaria)
Artime 65', 77'
Pirri 67'

15 July 1966
19:30 BST
Spain 2 – 1 Switzerland
Hillsborough Stadium, Sheffield
Attendance: 32,000
Referee: Tofik Bakhramov (Soviet Union)
Sanchís 57', Amancio 75'
Quentin 31'

16 July 1966
15:00 BST
Argentina 0 – 0 West Germany
Villa Park, Birmingham
Attendance: 51,000
Referee: Konstantin Zečević (Yugoslavia)

19 July 1966
19:30 BST
Argentina 2 – 0 Switzerland
Hillsborough Stadium, Sheffield
Attendance: 31,000
Referee: Joaquim Campos (Portugal)
Artime 52', Onega 79'

20 July 1966
19:30 BST
West Germany 2 – 1 Spain
Villa Park, Birmingham
Attendance: 51,000
Referee: Armando Marques (Brazil)
Emmerich 39', Seeler 84'
Fusté 23'

GROUP 3

Team	Pld	W	D	L	GF	GA	GAv	Pts
Portugal	3	3	0	0	9	2	4.50	6
Hungary	3	2	0	1	7	5	1.40	4
Brazil	3	1	0	2	4	6	0.67	2
Bulgaria	3	0	0	3	1	8	0.13	0

12 July 1966 19:30 BST
Brazil 2 – 0 Bulgaria
Goodison Park, Liverpool
Attendance: 48,000
Referee: Kurt Tschenscher (West Germany)
Pelé 15', Garrincha 63'

13 July 1966 19:30 BST
Portugal 3 – 1 Hungary
Old Trafford, Manchester
Attendance: 37,000
Referee: Leo Callaghan (Wales)
José Augusto 1', 67', Torres 90'
Bene 60'

15 July 1966
19:30 BST
Hungary 3 – 1 Brazil
Goodison Park, Liverpool
Attendance: 52,000
Referee: Ken Dagnall (England)
Bene 2', Farkas 64', Mészöly 73' (pen.)
Tostão 14'

16 July 1966
15:00 BST
Portugal 3 – 0 Bulgaria
Old Trafford, Manchester
Attendance: 26,000
Referee: José María Codesal (Uruguay)
Vutsov 17' (o.g.), Eusébio 38', Torres 81'

19 July 1966
19:30 BST
Portugal 3 – 1 Brazil
Goodison Park, Liverpool
Attendance: 62,000
Referee: George McCabe (England)
Simöes 15', Eusébio 27', 85'
Rildo 70'

20 July 1966 19:30 BST
Hungary 3 – 1 Bulgaria
Old Trafford, Manchester
Attendance: 22,000
Referee: Robert Goicoechea (Argentina)
Davidov 43' (o.g.), Mészöly 45', Bene 54'
Asparuhov 15'

GROUP 4

Team	Pld	W	D	L	GF	GA	GAv	Pts
Soviet Union	3	3	0	0	6	1	6.00	6
Korea DPR	3	1	1	1	2	4	0.50	3
Italy	3	1	0	2	2	2	1.00	2
Chile	3	0	1	2	2	5	0.40	1

12 July 1966
19:30 BST
Soviet Union 3 – 0 Korea DPR
Ayresome Park, Middlesbrough
Attendance: 22,000
Referee: Juan Gardeazábal Garay (Spain)
Malofeyev 31', 88', Banishevskiy 33'

13 July 1966
19:30 BST
Italy 2 – 0 Chile
Roker Park, Sunderland
Attendance: 30,000
Referee: Gottfried Dienst (Switzerland)
Mazzola 8', Barison 88'

15 July 1966
19:30 BST
Chile 1 – 1 Korea DPR
Ayresome Park, Middlesbrough
Attendance: 16,000
Referee: Ali Kandil (United Arab Republic)
Marcos 26' (pen.)
Pak Seung-Zin 88'

16 July 1966
15:00 BST
Soviet Union 1 – 0 Italy
Roker Park, Sunderland
Attendance: 27,800
Referee: Rudolf Kreitlein (West Germany)
Chislenko 57'

19 July 1966 19:30 BST
Korea DPR 1 – 0 Italy
Ayresome Park, Middlesbrough
Attendance: 18,000
Referee: Pierre Schwinte (France)
Pak Doo-Ik 42'

20 July 1966
19:30 BST
Soviet Union 2 – 1 Chile
Roker Park, Sunderland
Attendance: 22,000
Referee: John Adair (Northern Ireland)
Porkujan 28', 85'
Marcos 32'

ENGLAND '66

KNOCKOUT STAGE

QUARTER-FINALS

23 July 1966
15:00 BST
Portugal 5 – 3 Korea DPR
Goodison Park, Liverpool
Attendance: 51,780
Referee: Menachem Ashkenazi (Israel)
Eusébio 27', 43' (pen.), 56', 59' (pen.),
José Augusto 80'
Pak Seung-Zin 1', Lee Dong-Woon 22',
Yang Sung-Kook 25'

23 July 1966
15:00 BST
West Germany 4 – 0 Uruguay
Hillsborough Stadium, Sheffield
Attendance: 34,000
Referee: Jim Finney (England)
Haller 11', 83', Beckenbauer 70',
Seeler 75'

23 July 1966
15:00 BST
Soviet Union 2 – 1 Hungary
Roker Park, Sunderland
Attendance: 22,100
Referee: Juan Gardeazábal Garay (Spain)
Chislenko 5', Porkujan 46'
Bene 57'

23 July 1966
15:00 BST
England 1 – 0 Argentina
Wembley Stadium, London
Attendance: 90,000
Referee: Rudolf Kreitlein (West Germany)
Hurst 78'

SEMI-FINALS

25 July 1966 19:30 BST
West Germany 2 – 1 Soviet Union
Goodison Park, Liverpool
Attendance: 38,300
Referee: Concetto Lo Bello (Italy)
Haller 42', Beckenbauer 67'
Chislenko 47'

26 July 1966
19:30 BST
England 2 – 1 Portugal
Wembley Stadium, London
Attendance: 95,000
Referee: Pierre Schwinte (France)
B. Charlton 30', 80'
Eusébio 82' (pen.)

THIRD PLACE MATCH

28 July 1966 19:30 BST
Portugal 2 – 1 Soviet Union
Wembley Stadium, London
Attendance: 88,000
Referee: Ken Dagnall (England)
Eusébio 12' (pen.), Torres 89'
Malofeyev 43'

FINAL

30 July 1966 15:00 BST
England 4 – 2 West Germany (after extra time)
Wembley Stadium, London
Attendance: 98,000
Referee: Gottfried Dienst (Switzerland)
Hurst 18', 101', 120', Peters 78'

Haller 12', Weber 89'
1966 FIFA World Cup Winners:
England (First Title)